HANDWRITING PRACTICE 1

Children's Reading & Writing Education Books

All Rights reserved. No part of this book may be reproduced or used in any way or form or by any means whether electronic or mechanical, this means that you cannot record or photocopy any material ideas or tips that are provided in this book

Copyright 2016

Trace the letters and rewrite the words in the space provided.

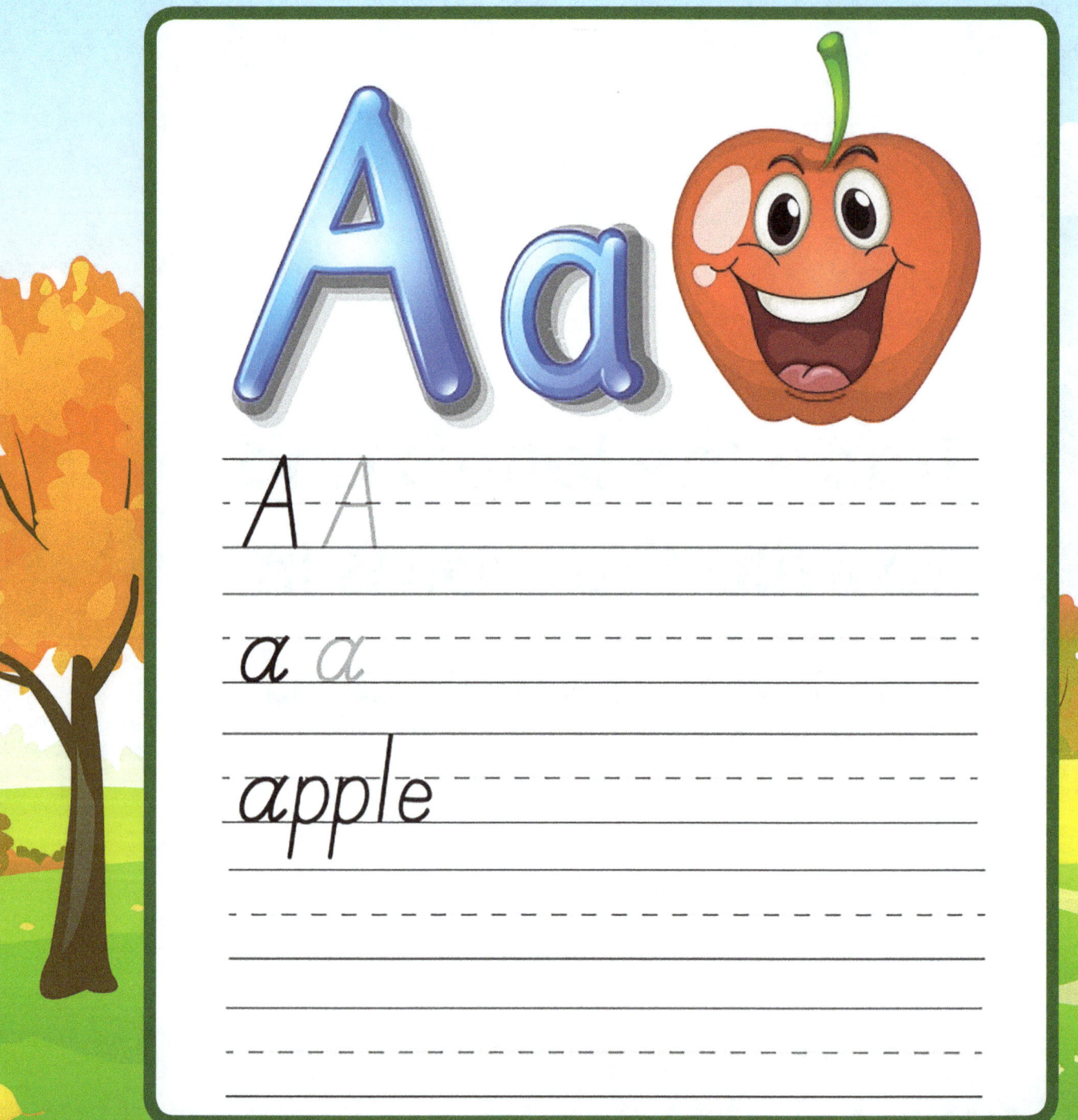

B b

B B

b b

bee

E E

e e

elephant

G G

g g

giraffe

N N

n n

nest

P p

P P

p p

panda

R R

r r

robot

U U

u u

umbrella

Y Y

y y

yacht

Trace the numbers and rewrite the words in the space provided.

Color the images.

number exercise

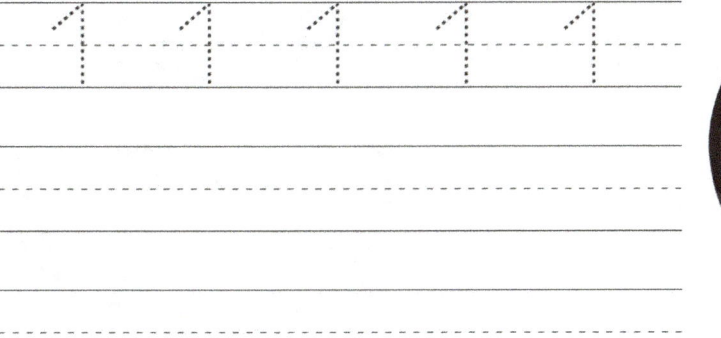 One

number exercise

2 Two

2 2 2 2 2

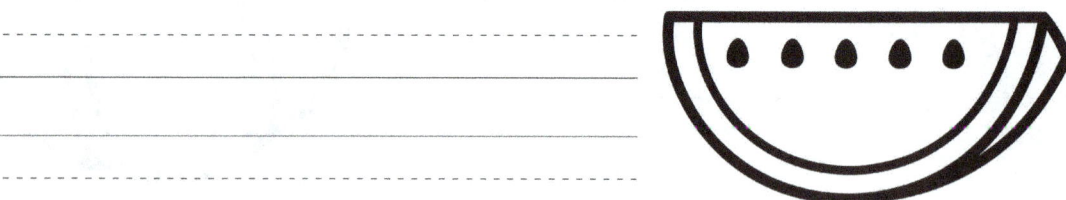

number exercise

number exercise

 Four

number exercise

5 **Five**

5 5 5 5 5

number exercise

6 Six

6 6 6 6 6

number exercise

7 Seven

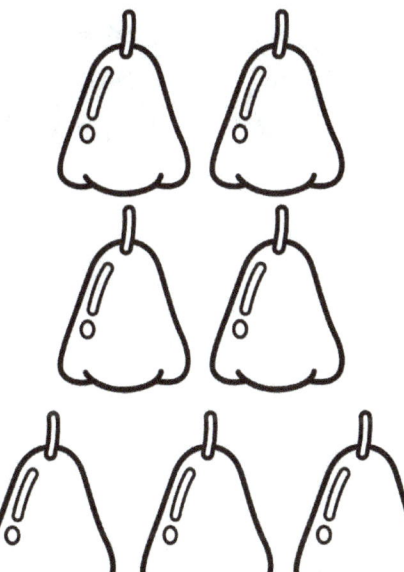

number exercise

8 Eight

www.ingramcontent.com/pod-product-compliance
Lightning Source LLC
LaVergne TN
LVHW061323060426
835507LV00019B/2268